GDAŃSK
The City of My Dreams

GDAŃSK, The City of My Dreams

Authors:	**Krzysztof Berenthal, Stanisław Sikora, Edward Klamann**
Photographs:	**Stanisław Składanowski,**
	Zbigniew Kosycarz (p. 17), **Janusz Rydzewski** (p. 22),
	Maciej Kostun (p. 50 and 120), **National Museum in Gdańsk** (p. 97)
Postcards:	**Krzysztof Berenthal**
Illustrations:	**Krzysztof Berenthal, Castle Museum at Malbork**
Photo Editor:	**Bogumiła Piazza**
Translation:	**BABEL, Sopot**
Computer layout:	**STUDIO JUSTA Gdańsk**

© **TESSA. tel. 0-600 075 458, fax (058) 552 20 97; e-mail: tessa@wydawnictwo.com.pl**

ISBN 83-88882-15-5

View of Gdańsk from Bishop's Hill (Biskupia Górka)

The name Gdańsk was first recorded in 999 by the biographer of St. Adalbert (św. Wojciech), the Benedictine monk Jan Kanapariusz, as Gyddanyzc, which stems from the old Slavic name of Gdaniesk. Both of these names are derived from the prefix gd- which indicates "wetness" or "dampness". The settlement which was the beginning of today's city was on the marshy terrain along the passageway across the former arm of the Vistula (Wisła) River, which is currently known as the Motława River. The name of this river undoubtedly comes from the now-extinct Prussian language (1283 - Mutulava). The alteration in the name could have occurred in the thirteenth century when large

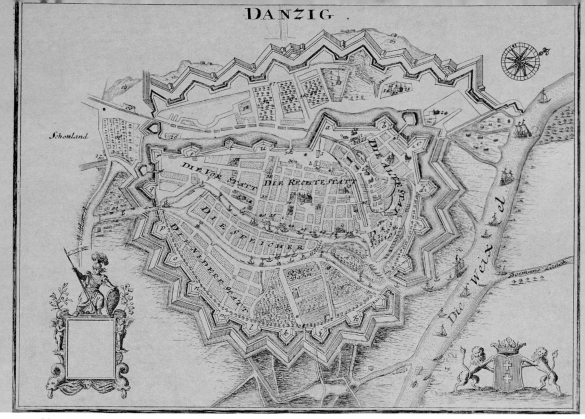

Map of the city, eighteenth century

numbers of Prussians settled in Gdańsk seeking the protection of Prince Świętopełek from the Teutonic Knights. The German name Danzig, however, is the transformation and vulgarization of the original word Gdańsk (1148 - Kdanzc, 1263 - Danzk, 1311 - Danczk, 1399 - Danczik, 1645 - Dantzigk).

The oldest traces of inhabitance were found in the Oliwa area and date from 2500-1700 BC. During the Roman era (early first century AD to 375), the area was visited by traders from the south in search of so-called "Baltic gold" or amber, and later, from the seventh to the ninth centuries, Arab traders even found their way here. It was in the ninth century that Gdańsk was established as an agricultural, craft and fishing settlement of about 300 inhabitants in the area of the Long Market (Długi Targ). In approximately 975, possibly on the initiative of Prince Mieszko I who ruled the Vistula Coastal (Pomorze Nadwiślańskie) area, as is documented in the Dagome iudex act of 991, a stronghold with a fishing and craft settlement was established just to the north of the initial settlement. It was from this stronghold that, for nearly two centuries, the rulers maintained control over the port adjacent to it, and, thus, the sailing traffic on the Vistula (Wisła) River. In 997, St Adalbert (św. Wojciech) Sławnikowic took it upon himself to go and, as Kanapariusz writes, "... fight the Prussian gods and statues, as the land was in close vicinity and was known from the memoirs of Prince" (Bolesław Chrobry). Thus acquainted with his wishes, the prince gave Adalbert a boat and 30 armed men to assure him a safe journey. Adalbert arrived first in Gdańsk (primo urbem Gyddanyzc), which lay on the border of the prince's vastest holdings on the sea coast. Here, by the mercy of God who had provided for his safe passage, Adalbert christened a large crowd of people. This probably took place on Easter Saturday 27 March 997.

Subisław was a descendent of the area's governors mentioned earlier, and was the first in the dynasty of east-Pomeranian princes based in Gdańsk who fought with Pomeranians, Danes, Prussians, Brandenburgers and Teutonic Knights in defense of the city. The greatest of these princes was Święto-pełk I, also known later as the Great (ca. 1220-1266), who, in definitively severing ties with the sovere-ignty of the Piast princes, made significant contributions to the development of Gdańsk. In approxima-tely 1227, he granted Gdańsk a city charter under Lübeck law, and brought the Dominican order from Kraków in order to strengthen the still weak hold Christianity had on his land. Under the rule of his son, Mściwoj I (1266-1294), whose political position was significantly weaker that of his father's, a strong city government in Gdańsk was created and its deputies (consules) are first mentioned in the historical record in 1274. In 1296, as stipulated by the Kępno treaty of 1284, following the death of Mściwoj (1294) the eastern Pomeranian principality came under the rule of Prince Przemysł of Greater Poland (Wielko-polska), later Przemysław II, King of Poland. The Gdańsk Pomorze area was involved in the insidious occupation of arming the Teutonic Knights in 1308-1309, thus contributing to the ouster of the lawful ruler, Prince Łokietek of the Brzesko-kujawska area. It was under his reign that the seal of the city bearing the inscription Sigillum burgensium in Dantzike was first used in 1299. During Teutonic times, the multi-partite character of the city's urban plan was consolidated, and three distinct and independent bodies existed side by side. These were the Main Town (Główne Miasto - also known as the Right Town (Prawe Miasto) from "the town on the right") including the Old Suburb (Stare Przedmieścia), the Old Town (Stare Miasto) and the New Town (Młode Miasto). The most economically powerful of the three, the Main Town, had approximately 10,000 inhabitants, and after receiving limited Lübeck law in 1342, surrounded itself with moats and defensive walls and began its most important building projects - the city hall and St. Mary's Church. In 1361, city representatives first took part in a meeting of the League of Hanseatic Cities; Gdańsk would play an important role in the organization for the next several centuries. After Teutonic rule had been overthrown, the Gdańsk region accepted Polish sovereignty and was incorporated into Poland in 1454, thus obtaining advantageous privileges from King Kazimierz Jagielloń-czyk which permitted unprecedented development and the legal ownership of approximately 1,000 km2 of outlying terrain. This was in return for the significant political, military and especially financial support the city gave to Poland during the so-called Thirteen Year War with the Teutonic Order (1454-1466). Over the course of barely a century, the city was transformed from one whose principal activity was trading grain and forestry products into Poland's main port, its shipbuilding center and its largest city with a population of approximately 20,000 citizens in 1460. Gdańsk maintained numerous contacts with the most important economic and financial centers throughout Europe.

At the beginning of the sixteenth century, Gdańsk, with a population of about 36-37 thousand inhabitants, quickly accepted the new religious ideas that were sweeping across western Europe, namely Lutheranism and Calvinism, and Catholicism became the minority faith. Under the influences of the Reformation and western Europe, patrician culture and art were shaped and the city took on a democra-tic atmosphere. The Gothic style gave way to the Renaissance and northern European Mannerism beca-me popular under the influence of the Netherlands. In the second half of the century, the population of Gdańsk had reached approximately 50,000 and included immigrants from Franconia, Rhineland, Bran-denburg and other German lands; there were also new citizens from Holland, England, Scotland, France and Italy. The tolerant religious climate of the city coupled with the patronage of the city and its patri-cians meant that thousands of superb artists (ca. 3,150 masters - in Kraków there were 714 at this time) and craftsmen (ca. 20,000) found employment in the city, especially during the so-called golden age from 1580 to 1650. Thanks to their efforts some of the most exquisite works in Poland and Europe were created. Simultaneously, many architectural projects were carried out including municipal buildings, over 300 granaries, beautiful residences and monumental fortifications whose rings of ramparts, bastions

Upland Gate (Brama Wyżynna), ca. 1880

Long Market (Długi Targ), ca. 1920

and moats surrounded the entire city. Residential developments were begun in the lower terrain that lay to the east of the historic city which became known as the Lower City (Dolne Miasto). By the mid-seventeenth century Gdańsk had become the largest metropolis in the Baltic Sea basin with a population of almost 77,000. The city's allegiance to Poland was expressed by its citizens when the Commonwealth was under the greatest threat. During the first Polish-Swedish war (1625-1629), the city was especially loyal when it did not allow the attackers to penetrate its wall and in thanks received special commendations from the Parliament on three occasions in 1626, 1628, and 1629. One of them was for the Battle of

Long Street (Ulica Długa) viewed through the Golden Gate (Złota Brama), 1920s

9

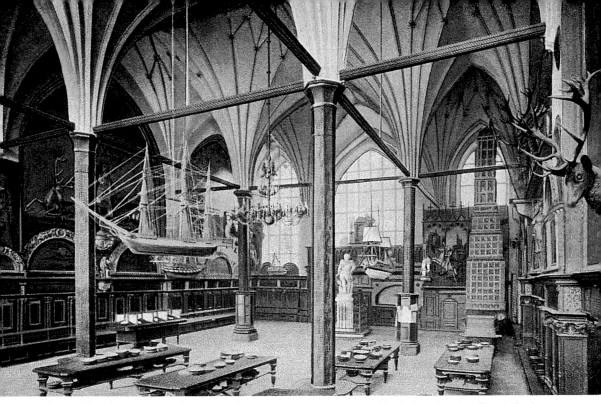

Interior of Artus Court (Dwór Artusa), early twentieth century. Business meetings and social gatherings of the city's elite took place here.

Oliwa in which the Gdańsk navy defeated the Swedish flotilla near Jelitkowo in the Gulf of Gdańsk on 28 November 1627. During the second war with Sweden (1655-1660), Gdańsk (along with Zamość and Jasna Góra in Częstochowa) again refused to surrender to the aggressors. The anniversary of the Polish-Swedish peace treaty, signed on 3 May 1660, was designated as an annual holiday and was even celebrated after Poland had been partitioned. Another dramatic event took place when the city defended King Stanisław Leszczyński, who was hiding within its walls, as Russian and Saxon armies laid siege to it from

Great Hall (Wielka Sień) in the **Main Town Hall (Ratusz Głównomiejski)**, late nineteenth century

Long Quay (Długie Pobrzeże). This port, the oldest on the Motława River, operated until the late 1940s.

early February to early July 1734. During this time, several hundred citizens were killed, approximately 1,800 residences were destroyed and over 100 granaries were burned.

Despite the severity of these events, Gdańsk's worst days were yet to come. During the first partition of Poland, the city lost its outlying terrain, Hel and Szkarpawa. Joanna Schopenhauer wrote of the Prussian King Frederick II "...he is a vampire which sucks the life blood from the city..." as he forced the city into almost total economic collapse by the imposition of embargoes. Although the city made persistent diplomatic attempts to avoid falling under Prussian rule, the expense was so high that the inevitable occurred in 1793. The new rulers revoked nearly all the privileges that had been bestowed

Beer Street (Ulica Piwna) and **St. Mary's Church (Kościół Mariacki)**, ca. 1920

Old Packing House (Stara Pakownia) on the bank of the Nowa Motława (early twentieth century). The picturesque port was full of ships, barges and rafts.

upon the city by the Polish kings. Economic stagnation and other problems slowly began to drive the city's citizens away, and its population fell to barely 36,000. Hope among the remaining residents of Gdańsk was rekindled in late May 1807 when, after a two-month siege, the French army marched into the city. The status of free city was given to Gdańsk under the Treaty of Tylża that was signed by Emperor Napoleon Bonaparte. After the emperor's defeat at Moscow and a siege that lasted nearly eight months, the Napoleon Army, including Polish legionnaires, left Gdańsk in early January 1813. Under the agreements of the Vienna Congress of 1815, Gdańsk was returned to the Prussians. There was a certain degree of economic recovery in the second half of the nineteenth century especially after the opening of the railway lines between Gdańsk and Tczew in 1852 and Gdańsk and Szczecin in 1870. Industry slowly began to grow; the turnover in the commercial port, which was moved from the Motława River to New Port (Nowy Port), increased, shipbuilding began to develop

Oliwa. A district of Gdańsk in the early twentieth century, Oliwa had once been a small village adjacent to the Cistercian monastery, later a civil parish and a health resort. It is famed for its park and organ. Famous church and Kashubian fairs also took place here, and it was the starting point for pilgrimages to Kalwaria Wejherowska.

at the Klawitter Shipyard, and other branches of industry, principally armaments, began to expand. At the close of the nineteenth century, large-scale works were undertaken to dismantle the fortifications to the north and west of the city. This allowed for the re-development of the transportation system and enlarged the area available for residential building. Despite strong Germanization, the Polish identity survived in Gdańsk and many Polish religious, cultural and educational and other organizations were founded.

Gdańsk had about 175,000 residents in 1914, 15% of them Poles, but population growth was much slower here than in other cities in the country of the Hohenzollerns. From the defeat of the Germans in

1918, a new hope was born among Poles that Gdańsk would return to the newly reborn Commonwealth. The dilatory politics of the great powers, especially England, with regard to Germany destroyed these efforts. The Free City of Gdańsk was established under the Treaty of Versailles as a protectorate of the League of Nations to be represented by the High Commissioner. Approximately 356,000 residents (19% of them of Polish heritage) lived in this area of 1,893 km2 that stretched from Gdynia in the north almost to Tczew in the south. The complicated administrative structure of this "artificial creature" led to 70 legal and political confrontations between Poland and Gdańsk. Many of these were played out on the international stage, and as a result Polish-German relations were under constant strain, with Poland's western neighbor unable to accept the loss of Gdańsk. As soon as Hitler came to power in 1933, anti-Polish sentiment in Gdańsk began to grow with the spread of Fascism. The slogan " Return to the Reich" (zurück zum Reich) became the main propaganda theme of Gdańsk's German residents who directed their hatred mainly towards Polish railway workers, customs officers and postal employees. Despite the brutal fight against the Polish identity, it persevered thanks to the extraordinary efforts of the Gdańsk Polonia in the spheres of education, culture, science, religion, politics, propaganda and social and economic issues. September 1, 1939, the day on which the city's Fascist-controlled Senate illegally annexed the Free City to the Reich, was tragic for many Gdańsk citizens of Polish heritage who were either arrested and placed in concentration camps, expelled, or forced to emigrate. The Polish Post Office, whose 39 defenders were murdered, and Westerplatte, which was defended for almost seven days, became symbols of Polish bravery. When the war turned against the Germans and the front drew nearer to the coast, orders were received from Hitler's Headquarters on 26 March 1945 to change Gdańsk into a fortress. After a bloody and vicious four-day fight, the Soviet Army took the city. The historic center of the city had literally disappeared from the face of the earth with 90% of it in ruins. Of 12,600 buildings, 60% were completely destroyed and more than 57,000 flats had ceased to exist; there was no electricity, gas or transportation. Many industrial operations were devastated as the liberating Soviet troops cleared out any of the machines, equipment and tools that had escaped destruction. The Soviets continued their criminal behavior as they planned and systematically destroyed the surviving quarters.

Life in Gdańsk, however, was not fully extinguished; by 6 April 1945 the city had a president followed by the first issue of the daily newspaper Dziennik Bałtycki on 19 May. A census taken on 16 June showed that 8,000 Poles and 124,000 Germans, most of whom had been forced to emigrate by 1946, were living in Gdańsk. The costly operation to clear up the 3 million m3 of rubble began almost immediately and a few years later rebuilding began which has continued uninterrupted until today.

Long Market (Długi Targ), 1945. The historic center of Gdańsk (both the Main and Old Towns) were over 90% destroyed. Only one church and several buildings had not been burned or shelled.

The rebuilding of Gdańsk was not an issue that had been decided from the start. In writing the word "rebuilt", I am thinking more about today's urban form and historic atmosphere which can be found in reconstructed and stylized buildings.

The original concept of reconstructing Gdańsk's historical center was to clear away the rubble, level the remaining buildings and to replace it with architecture in the spirit of social realism. The Main

City was to have been partially planted with trees to create a kind of park dotted with enclaves of preserved, historic architecture, such as St. Mary's Church (Kościół Mariacki), Artus Court (Dwór Artusa), and the Old Town Hall (Ratusz Staromiejski). Surrounding this, new housing estates were to have been built, like those in the Warsaw districts Praga II or MDM. The architecture in Wrzeszcz was also to have been significantly changed; for example, a housing estate like MDM was to have been built near the train station, a building of gigantic proportions, similar to Warsaw's Palace of Culture and Science (Pałac Kultury i Nauki) was to have been erected at the intersection of ul. Partyzantów and ul. Grunwaldzka. Fortunately, the planned demolition of the old buildings was never realized, and only a small fragment of a promenade, today's ul. Klonowa, and some buildings were realized. Political changes which occurred after 1954 allowed for the concept of Gdańsk's reconstruction to be changed and a new urban plan was developed, but this time, the city's cultural elite had much more influence on it.Waves of new residents continuously poured into Gdańsk in search of work, a roof over their heads or simply their niche in the world. Many of them came from the former Polish territories in the east, especially from the vicinity of Vilnius and, to a lesser extent, from Lviv. Among Gdańsk's growing population were a significant number of intellectuals including artists, scientists and art critics and historians. Many of them arrived with the love of their former eastern hometowns and bestowed it upon the new city just emerging from a sea of rubble. Throughout the disastrous postwar period, when first the Soviet Red Army senselessly burned the city to the ground and several Polish authorities praised the destruction by saying "...finally the nest of Germanization and Drang nach Osten has been annihilated ...", Gdańsk also had some luck. The city was inhabited by intelligent people who grew to truly love it. It was they who were ultimately successful in convincing the state authorities that Gdańsk should be reconstructed to avoid criticism from the world that all traces of the German presence in the city had been eradicated. They saved the historical nucleus of the city. The first postwar guide to Gdańsk was written by Jan Kilarski, the author of the beautiful prewar Gdańsk monograph in the Polish Miracles (Cuda Polski) series. Reading this guidebook, one can wander the city streets and admire its beautiful monuments as if they were standing; in reality, the city lay in ruins.

Reconstruction began in the early 1950s in the Main City quarter between ul. Ogarna, ul. Garbary and ul. Długa. Several public buildings were erected - the post-office and the Leningrad cinema - and old buildings that had survived, including the city hall, the St. George shooting range (strzelnica św. Jerzego), and a majority of churches, were either secured or their reconstruction was begun. Work in earnest, however, did not begin until the urban plan, which outlined building priorities and introduced new transportation solutions, had been developed and approved in 1960.

Within ten years, the basic outline of the Main City had been rebuilt, and the majority the destruction in Wrzeszcz, Oliwa, Nowy Port and other city districts had been repaired.

The first building in the new Przymorze residential district, which was built using traditional brick construction, was completed in 1960. Soon after, preparations were made for the creation of the huge Przymorze housing estate, the so-called "bedroom of Gdańsk", which became a symbol of socialist house-building. Architects competed in creating ever larger buildings and this spurred the creation of the wave-shaped (falowiec) apartment blocks, thus named for their long, undulating facades. The first such buildings were small - only 350 m long - but later they reached lengths of up to 850 m. The empty spaces between Old Oliwa and the Baltic Sea shore were slowly filled in, and the area which had once served for Prussian army maneuvers became a testing ground for architects and builders.

Combining the celebrations of Poland's millenium with the anniversary of ten centuries of Gdańsk secured new funds from the central budget for renovations and investments in the city, including the reconstruction of the Great Mill (Wielki Młyn), the Crane (Żuraw) and other buildings, and the renovation of the train station. The city's transportation system was also rebuilt, and new roads, like the so-called "Trasa W-Z" and Podwale Przedmiejskie, were created, and the Piastowski Junction was modernized along with Błędnik Bridge.

Universities and research institutions came to play an important role in the development of the city. By the end of the 1960s, Gdańsk had six institutions of higher education, five research institutions and 26 branches and departments of research and development institutions. The Gdańsk Technical University and the Medical Academy occupied the leading positions. At this time in Gdańsk, there was a total of 15,000 students, and it was this numerous and free-thinking group that initiated the violent protests of March 1968. The communist authorities effectively used propaganda to turn the workers against the students. The incidents of 1970 took a completely different turn, and although the core group of protesters was the shipyard workers, many students and some intellectuals joined in the clashes that lasted for three days. On Wednesday, 16 December, the situation changed dramatically after five shipyard workers were killed in front of the Gdańsk Shipyard gate; the strikes ended but tensions remained high. Relative peace was established when Edward Gierek, the new First Secretary of the Central Committee of the Polish Worker's Party (PZPR), visited in January 1971, and the government reversed their decision to hike food prices.

The August strikes released unprecedented power, courage and hope in the citizens of Gdańsk. Outdoor masses held at Gate 2 drew thousands of people to both sides of the fence; access to the shipyard for non-employees was only by permission of the Inter-factory Strike Committee (MKS). The masses were not only an expression of spontaneous religious feeling, but were also a demonstration of the power of the rebellious public.

The euphoria of victory following the signing by the authorities of the so-called August Agreements (Porozumienia Sierpniowe) that ended the strike and, among other points, agreed to legalize the Solidarność Independent Trade Union (Niezależne Związki Zawodowe). At the time, it was the only institution in opposition to the communist authorities that was legal.

Discontinuing the dialogue with the people and the declaration of martial law were aimed at crushing the backbone of democratic opposition. Common acts of violence and the humiliation of ordinary citizens by intervention forces, especially by the militarized police (ZOMO), were symbolized by the police breaking into striking factories (Gate 2 at the Gdańsk Shipyard) and beating and killing strikers.

During the 1970's, there was a virtual storm of ideas in Gdańsk concerning modern architecture and urban development in the city center. Fortunately, the majority of them were never realized, altho-

The pilgrimage of John Paul II to Poland in June 1987 revived the hope of the Polish people. His visit to Gdańsk was an important part of the pilgrimage, and the mass held in the Zaspa housing estate for nearly a million faithful from Gdańsk and other parts of Poland was a great experience. The fabulous, monumental altar in the shape of a galleon, designed by Marian Kołodziej and Lech Zaleski, carried its own special symbolism.

ugh some have still not died and continue to haunt like poltergeists. One of them is the 1960s - 1970s concept of the north-south route called the Red Road (Czerwona Droga) that disregards all existing historical and geographical realities. This spirit is still present among city planners and has destructive impact on the development of the city.

The closing of the civilian and military airport in Wrzeszcz and its move to the village of Rębiechowo, 10 km from the city, was not only a necessary move, but also a wise one. The terrain of the former airport became the site of the massive Zaspa housing estate. According to its planners, the new design of Zaspa was to have become a model for housing estates throughout Poland. In practice, another concrete bedroom was created.

The late 1970s were turbulent times in the Tri-Cities, and signals from Radom and Ursus fueled an already hot atmosphere. Flowers were laid and meetings were held in front of Gdańsk Shipyard Gate 2 each December, and manifestations on 11 November became a tradition. Therefore, the strike that broke out on 14 August 1980 was the rather logical consequence of earlier events. The atmosphere in the city at this time was akin to that during the Warsaw Uprising; everybody felt like pitching in and helping. Spontaneously, the shipyard was fully supplied with food, paper and other necessary items. A collection box for funds to build a Monument to the Fallen Shipyard Workers (Pomnik Poległych Stoczniowców) stood in front of the shipyard gates and every passer-by felt obliged to contribute. Negotiations between the newly formed trade unions (Międzyzakładowy Komitet Strajkowy), the only body representing the strikers, and the authorities were broadcast first on the shipyard's public address system and then on local radio. The day the agreements with the government delegation were signed was one of great happiness, despite the fact that many people doubted the lasting power of the documents. This feeling became increasingly strong as it appeared that the only tangible achievement of the August strikes was the monument that was quickly growing in front of Gate 2. Although 13 December 1981 was a sunny day, martial law engulfed the city like a black cloud that darkened many people's lives for almost five years. The anguish of the first half of the 1980s was compensated for by the visit of Pope John Paul II to Gdańsk on 11 June 1987. The hope and happiness which the Pope instilled in the people of Gdańsk had to suffice for many years to come.

The most recent important event to take place in Gdańsk was the celebration of its millenium in 1997. The festivities lasted for almost a year and were as much applauded as maligned. A plan for the reconstruction and revitalization of Granary Island was approved in 1998; it is the third such plan since 1947 for the island still covered by rubble. The only effective realization in this area is the adaptation of the former electro-heating plant on Ołowianka Island as the new headquarters of the philharmonic orchestra.

The Renaissance **Upland Gate** (**Brama Wyżynna**) at ul. Wały Jagiellońskie is the beginning of the so-called Royal Route (Droga Królewska). Until the end of the nineteenth century, the gate was part of an enormous earthen and brick fortification wall to the west of which was a wide, deep moat. The gate, which guarded the main entrance to the city, was designed and built by Hans Kramer in 1574-1576. Its stone decorations, by Wilhelm van den Block in 1586-1588, included rustication and a frieze above the entablature with large crests of the Royal Prussians, Poland (with the Bull-calf or *Ciołek* crest of the Poniatowski family) and Gdańsk (the Hohenzollern crest was added on the eastern side in 1884. There are three Latin inscriptions beneath the crests; the middle one reads *Justice and piety are the foundations of all states*. The Gothic buildings of the Przedbramie (literally - the area in front of the gate) to Long Street (ul. Długa) are visible in the background.

The **Przedbramie** (literally - the area in front of the gate) to Long Street (ul. Długa) is a medieval defensive complex that dates from the second half of the fourteenth century and was once an extension of the Long Street Gate (Brama Długouliczna) on the western side. It was expanded in the fifteenth and sixteenth centuries and transformed into a municipal prison at the end of the sixteenth century. Designed by Antoni van Obberghen and constructed by Jan Strakowski, it consists of the **Torture House (Katownia)**, with a reconstructed top, on the western side and the **Prison Tower (Wieża Więzienna)**, with its reconstructed cupola, that are connected by walls that form an internal courtyard. Part of the stone work from the destroyed St. James' Gate (Brama św. Jakuba) was used in the western wall of the Katownia, and decorative elements from destroyed townhouses were used in the northern wall on the courtyard side. The entrance which leads to the pillory's hanging bridge in the eastern wall of the Wieża Więzienna has been preserved. Today, part of the complex houses the Court and Law Museum of Gdańsk (Muzeum Sądownictwa i Prawa Gdańskiego) and the Museum of Amber is in the planning stages. The Golden Gate (Złota Brama) stands in the background.

The Renaissance **Golden Gate (Złota Brama)** on the right adjoins the Gothic Court of the **St. George Brotherhood (Dwór Bractwa św. Jerzego)** on the left. The gate, a wonderful example of the Italian style, was constructed by Jan Strakowski according to the design by Abraham van den Block in 1612-1614. Eight allegorical figures made by Piotr Ringering in 1648 (reconstructed) adorn the attic of the gate on both sides and screen the roof. Among the Latin inscriptions on the gate, that from the side of ul. Długa reads *Small states grow in harmony - large states fall in discord.* The palace is an example of Flemish building. It was built partially on the defensive walls (ground floor- arms storage, first floor - meeting, fencing and reception rooms) and was designed by Hans Glotau in 1494 for the elite St. George Brotherhood. In the seventeenth century, the tent-like roof of the building was finished with a turret and a lamp (reconstructed) with a metal figure of St. George (copy, the original figure from 1556 is in the National Museum in Gdańsk).

The Millenium Tree (Drzewko Milenium), made of metal and decorated with symbolic gifts from Polish and foreign smiths, was erected on the Coal Market (Targ Węglowy) in 1997 to celebrate the Gdańsk Millenium. It was designed by Wojciech Schwartz and constructed by Leonard Dajkowski. The reconstructed high defensive wall covered by ivy is visible in the background. Only partially visible on the left is the **Straw Tower (Baszta Słomiana)** (fourteenth century) that is joined by a brick connector to the **Great Armory (Wielka Zbrojownia)** (not pictured).

The **Great Armory** (**Wielka Zbrojownia**) is one of the most valuable examples of Dutch Mannerist architecture in Poland. From the Coal Market (Targ Węglowy) it resembles the houses of rich Gdańsk merchants more than it does an armory, which it was until the nineteenth century. The **Straw Tower** (**Baszta Słomiana**) (fourteenth century), with its 4 m thick walls, was once used for gun powder storage and is adjacent to the **Great Armory** (**Wielka Zbrojownia**) and in line with the Gothic defensive wall. Further to the north is the **Wybrzeże Theater** (**Teatr Wybrzeże**) (not pictured) which was designed by Lech Kadłubowski and built in 1962-1966. Another interesting building is the **Old Pharmacy** (**Stara Apteka**) that dates from the first half of the seventeenth century.

The Beer Street (ul. Piwna) facade of the **Great Armory** (**Wielka Zbrojownia**) (1601-1609), designed by Antoni van Obberghen with stonework made by Abraham van den Block and Willem van der Meer (known as Bart the Younger), is a masterpiece of Dutch Mannerist architecture. Characteristic decorative elements include the four gables topped with figures of Gdańsk soldiers, side staircase towers, an alcove that houses a figure of Athena, portals and a shaft for retrieving ammunition from the basements. Looking from the Armory (Zbrojownia), there is a view of Beer Street (ul. Piwna - named after the many breweries that were once located here), whose dominating feature is **St. Mary's Church** (**Kościół Mariacki**). The first building on the right is one of the most beautiful Baroque townhouses in Gdańsk; currently it is called the **Craft House** (**Dom Rzemiosła** - ul. Piwna 1) and was built by Andrzej Schlüter the Elder in 1640.

The building of Gothic defensive fortifications, including moats, walls, bastions, and towers, began in 1343 with the Corner Bastion (**Baszta Narożna**) (to the left) that surrounded the Main Town. The **Scouts' House (Dom Harcerza)** complex is adjacent to the **Corner Bastion (Baszta Narożna)** on the east; it is composed of seventeenth century buildings that were adapted after WWII. The fully reconstructed Gothic **Schultz Bastion (Baszta Schultza)**, named after J. C. Schultz, a nineteenth century engraver and enthusiast of Gdańsk's architectural monuments, and the partly reconstructed Gothic **Brewery Bastion (Baszta Browarna)** from the fourteenth century, are visible farther on.

31

The Rococo **Fahrenheit House** (**Dom Fahrenheita** - ul. Ogarna 94) dates from ca. 1760. It was rebuilt in 1953-1954 and the facade was reconstructed in 1960. Daniel Gabriel Fahrenheit (1686-1736), who was born and raised in this building, constructed a mercury thermometer using his own temperature scale in which water boils at 212°F. Parallel to Long Street (ul. Długa) and Long Market (Długi Targ), Ogarna Street (ul. Ogarna - properly Psia or Dog) is closed on its eastern end at the Motława River by the fifteenth century Cow Gate (Brama Krowia) that has been reconstructed from its foundations.

Long Street (Ulica Długa - *longa platea*, 1331), commonly known as the "salon of Gdańsk", is a continuation of the Royal Route. The street curves slightly from the west, and the Main Town Hall (Ratusz Głównego Miasta) closes it on the northern wall and the Konert House (Dom Konerta) closes it on the southern side. At the far end of Long Market (Długi Targ), the extension of Long Street (ul. Długa), is the Green Gate (Zielona Brama) which closes the square. This street was almost entirely destroyed in 1945 and the townhouses that line it today are reconstructions that range from fifteenth century Gothic to twentieth century pseudo-classicist. The townhouse at number 71 is special thanks to the preserved late-Gothic profiles from the second half of the fifteenth century and the original Renaissance and Rococo elements that were added to the peak of the building. Until the late nineteenth century there were porches on both sides of the street, but they were removed in order to improve traffic and to make way for a streetcar line (subsequently removed in the 1960s).

The Rococo-Classicist **Uphagen House (Dom Uphagena** - ul. Długa 12) was erected in 1776 by Johann Beniamin Dreyer for the well-educated patrician Johann Uphagen, who, to protest the capture of Gdańsk by the Prussians, resigned his councilor's position in 1791. It was his will that the house become a museum, and following postwar reconstruction and the partial restoration of its interior decor, it has become one. The large windows of the facade are accentuated by the clear vertical and horizontal divisions. The house's triangular peak is framed by volutes which sweep downward from the pediment across the two upper stories. The ground-floor portal is exceptional due to the crest of the house's owner and his wife, Abigail, which is located in the transom window.

The high-ceilinged entrance-hall in the **Uphagen House (Dom Uphagena)** is a representative room which is characteristic for patrician homes in eighteenth century Gdańsk. Invited guests and clients were greeted in the hall and then the party would move to other richly decorated rooms either on the ground or the first floor. In this house, for example, they would go to the red room - the living room that was named after the color of its damask wall-covering.

The Renaissance **Ferber House** (**Dom Ferberów** - ul. Długa 28) was erected in 1560 by Mayor Konstanty Ferber, who was from a renowned patrician family. The building's facade is richly decorated with pilasters and friezes based on the best Italian architectural patterns. Near the peak of the house there are figures of famous antique characters, the crests of Poland, the Royal Prussians and Gdańsk appear in a lower frieze, and the lowest friezes depict busts of ancient heroes. The facade of the early Baroque **Czirenberg House** (**Dom Czirenberga**) from ca. 1620 was decorated with medallions depicting the heads of Roman emperors by Piotr Ringering (1674).

This Renaissance town-house was called the **Lion's Castle (Lwi Zamek** - ul. Długa 35) after the lion statues on the railings of the former porch. It was built by Hans Kramer in 1569 and was rich in sculptural decoration. A figure representing Fortune stands on the triangular peak, while the frieze in the reconstructed entrance-hall depicts Grammar, Arithmetic, Rhetoric and Geometry. It is here that the Schwartzwald family entertained King Władysław IV with a feast and dancing in 1636.

The southern frontage of Long Street (ul. Długa) is closed by a house dating from ca. 1560 known as the **Konert House (Dom Konerta)** after its first owner, or as the Schumann House (Dom Schumannów) after his heirs. It is regarded as one of the most beautiful patrician houses in Gdańsk. The classic motif of an entablature with a triglyph-metope frieze in which there are alternating rounded shields and bucrania is repeated on the three floors of the red facade. In defiance of the rule of superposition, these are supported only by Tuscan pilasters and garlands with figures of Greek gods (Zeus, Athena) at the top. Currently, the building is the headquarters of the Gdańsk Branch of the Polish Tourist Association (Oddział Gdańskiego Polskiego Towarzystwa Turystyczno-Krajoznawczego). A beautiful stone partition wall with three arcades above which there are bas-reliefs of Mercury, Juno and Neptune, and an entrance-hall, can currently be seen in the Old Town Hall (Ratusz Staromiejski).

The Gothic-Renaissance **Main Town Hall** (**Ratusz Głównego Miasta**), the headquarters of the city council and its offices, was the most important municipal building in old Gdańsk. It was built by Henryk Ungeradin in 1379-1381 and then later expanded and modernized in the century between the fifteenth - seventeenth centuries by Antoni van Oppberghen. Due to the preserved and reconstructed interiors such rooms as the Great Vestibule (Wielka Sień), the Great Hall of the Former Police-Administrative Court (Wielka Sala Wety), the Great Christopher Hall (Wielki Krzysztof), the Red Room (Sala Czerwona) - also known as the Great (Wielka) or Summer Council Hall (Letnia Sala Rady), the Winter (Zimowa) or Small Council Hall (Mała Sala Rady), the Small Hall of the Former Police-Administrative Court (Mała Sala Wety and Kamlaria), are all very interesting. Other rooms house both permanent and temporary exhibitions. This building was completely destroyed by fire and shell-marked in March 1945. After extensive reconstruction and renovation, it reopened on 1 April 1970 as the headquarters of the Gdańsk History Museum (Muzeum Historyczne Miasta Gdańska). Fragments of the frameworks of houses (ca. early fourteenth century) and defensive walls built by previous settlers have been discovered in the basements

The reconstructed Renaissance **dome** of the Main Town Hall (Ratusz Głównego Miasta) is 35 meters high, has three gloriettes and was made by the Gdańsk builder Dirk Daniels in 1561. The spire is topped by a large (2.03 m), gold-plated figure of King Zygmunt August (reconstructed), and four Jagiellonian eagles grace each of the corners. A reconstructed carillon hangs in the tower and replaces the one from 1560 by Johann Moor, the bell-founder from Brabandt. It is coupled with a clock that retains its original face. There is a beautiful view of the city and the surrounding areas from the top of the tower (48 m).

The **Red Room** (**Czerwona Sala** - named after the color of its damask wall-covering) in the Main Town Hall (Ratusz Głównego Miasta), was jointly designed by Hans Vredeman de Vries, the outstanding painter and theoretician of perspective, and the master wood-carver Szymon Herle in 1589-1591. They divided the interior decoration into three zones: the first includes the floors, the benches near the walls, the portal and the fireplace; the second is comprised of the lower molding and the frieze with its seven allegorical paintings; the third was made by Izaak van den Block, and includes the upper molding and the ceiling paintings framed in Herle's marvelous wood carvings. The famous painting *The Apotheosis of Gdańsk* (*Apoteoza Gdańska*) from 1608 is here.

The magnificent **fireplace** made by sculptor Willem van der Meer (Bart the Younger) in 1593 is in the Red Room (Czerwona Sala) of the Main Town Hall (Ratusz Głównego Miasta). It is regarded as one of the most valuable Renaissance pieces in Gdańsk. Its base consists of two muscular atlantes on either side of the fireplace that support the entablature with a Doric frieze. Centered in the middle is a polychromed and gold-plated cartouche with the crest of Gdańsk. The decoration of the fireplace is completed with inscriptions in Latin warning the citizens of the consequences of betraying their own city.

The massive and decorative entrance porches, known as przedproża, located on the southern wall of Long Market (Długi Targ) date from the seventeenth and eighteenth centuries. They served as meeting and resting places for the city's patricians in former times. The porches were largely destroyed in the second half of the nineteenth century, but surviving original stone elements were often employed in their reconstruction.

The **Long Market** (**Długi Targ** - name from the fifteenth century) is the eastern extension of Long Street (ul. Długa). Once oval in shape, it was rebuilt and widened at the end of the fourteenth century according to the design of Henryk Ungeradin. It became the city's representative square and a patrician forum, in which the most glamorous civic buildings and townhouses with porches were erected.

The **Royal Houses** (**Kamienice Królewskie** - ul. Długi Targ 1-4). From the right: a classicist house dating from ca. 1800; a Renaissance house with a figure of Neptune (first half of the seventeenth century); two Baroque houses (second half the of seventeenth and eighteenth centuries). Polish kings were entertained here, including Zygmunt III Waza (1623, 1626, 1627), Władysław IV (1635, 1636), Jan Kazimierz (1651, 1657, 1660), Jan III Sobieski (1677), August II Sas (1698) and Stanisław Leszczyński (1734). Prince Aleksander Sobieski was born on 9 September 1677 in the second house from the right.

The **Neptune Fountain** was designed by Abraham van den Block and the first versions of the base and the pool were made in his workshop in 1613. The figure of the Roman god of the Seas was probably sculpted by Peter Husen and cast in bronze by Gerd Benning and Ottomer Wittner in 1615. The fountain was put into operation in 1633. Its core is new, the grate with eagles and the Gdańsk crest is a reconstruction, the dish and the animal procession that accompany Neptune date from 1761 and were designed by Johann Carl Stender.

Artus Court (**Dwór Artusa** - ul. Długi Targ 44), originally the headquarters of the merchant brotherhoods, later the stock exchange and a museum, is a Gothic construction dating from 1476-1481 (the side on ul. Chlebnicka). The Mannerist facade, designed by Abraham van den Block in 1616-1617 is interesting because it retains the Gothic windows and rustication from 1552. Likenesses of King Zygmunt III Waza and his son Władysław decorate the portal. The interior of the monumental hall has a stellar-palm vaulted ceiling supported by four richly decorated columns (fifteenth -nineteenth centuries). The late-Baroque eighteenth century Jurors' Old House (Stary Dom Ławy) is to the left at number 45 and to the right side at number 43 is the Baroque Jurors' New House (Nowy Dom Ławy), also known as the Vestibule of Gdańsk (Sień Gdańska) because of its magnificent interior (seventeenth and eighteenth centuries). At the beginning of the twentieth century, it housed Lesser Giełdziński's collections of applied art.

49

The **tiled furnace** in the Artus Court (Dwór Artusa) was made in 1545-1546 by George Stelzener, the construction worker Wolf and the painter Jost. Reaching a height of 11 meters, the furnace was the tallest in Europe at the time. It is made of several hundred colorful tiles, with eleven doubled images of rulers (including German Emperor Charles V), allegorical figures, ornamental motifs and the well-known set of Polish, Royal Prussian and Gdańsk crests. Its reconstruction, which was completed in 1995, has been one of the greatest recent accomplishments of conservation work.

The **Golden House (Złota Kamienica** - ul. Długa 41), with its reconstructed upper part, is famous for the lavish gold-plated bas-reliefs of historical and legendary scenes, figures and ornamental decorations in the horizontal frieze above the entablature. Originally, the house was inhabited by Mayor Hans Speymann (thus the name **Speyman House (Dom Speymannów)**, and after 1786 it became known as the Steffens House (Dom Steffensów). It was designed by Abraham van den Block and decorated by Johann Voigt of Rostoka in 1618-1618. Among the famous rulers depicted in the plinths of the molding are two Polish kings - (Władysław Jagiełło and Zygmunt III Waza. Its facade was constructed according to the classic superposition order, with Tuscan pilasters at the ground level, Ionic on the first and second floors, Corinthian on the third floor, and Mannerist on the fourth floor.

The **Long Quay (Długie Pobrzeże)** is a stone (formerly wooden) landing pier several hundred meters long on the left bank of the Motława River. Along it are reconstructed patrician houses punctuated at intervals by defensive gates that close the streets perpendicular to the old port. These are the **Cow (Krowia)**, **Green (Zielona)**, **Chlebnicka**, **St. Mary (Mariacka)**, **Holy Ghost (Św. Ducha)**, **Crane (Żuraw)**, **St. John (Świętojańska)** and **Stall Keeper (Straganiarska) gates**, most of which date to the fifteenth century. Today it is a poplar promenade and Żegluga Gdańska SA operates a passenger ferry service near the **Green Bridge (Zielony Most** - formerly Kogi). On the opposite side Granary Island (Wyspa Spichrzów) and a warehouse from the interwar period are partially visible. Ołowianka Island is further in the distance.

A fragment of the Gothic **Stągiewna Gate (Brama Stągiewna)** is visible on Granary Island (Wyspa Spichlerzy) which is surrounded by the waters of the Old (Stara) and New (Nowa) Motława rivers. The gate consists of the lower **Stągiewka Bastion (Baszta Stągiewka**, ca. 1456) and the upper **Stągwi Bastion (Baszta Stągwi**, 1515). Beyond a newly built quarter of stylized townhouses (1997-1999) to the south of ul. Stągiewna is **Stągiewny Bridge (Most Stągiewny)** which stands next to the gate. The panorama of the Main and Old towns (Główne and Stare Miasto) up to the edge of the Gdansk Heights (Wysoczyzna Gdańska) opens up in the background.

The Gothic **Chlebnicka Gate** (**Brama Chlebnicka** - ca. 1450) closes ul. Chlebnicka and on its Motława side is adorned with the oldest crest of Gdańsk - two crosses without a crown. A stylized lily decorates the other side of the gate, and its second name, Lily Gate, is derived from this. Further along is the reconstructed **Naturalists House** (Dom Przyrodników), with its characteristic alcove, and the adjacent **St. Mary Gate** (**Brama Mariacka**).

54

The first house on the right is the late-Gothic **Schlieff House** (**Dom Schlieffów** - later **Lehmann House**) at ul. Chlebnicka 12 that dates from 1520, which can be seen from ul. Mariacka at the intersection of ul. Grząska. It is a full reconstruction as the original was disassembled in 1822 on the order of the Prussian King Frederick Wilhelm III and reconstructed on Peacock Island in Potsdam near Berlin, where it is known as Kavalierhaus. The fourth house in the row is the large **English House** (**Dom Angielski** - so-called as English merchants gathered here in the seventeenth century). It is also known as the **Angel House** (**Dom Pod Aniołami**) because of the decorative angel heads that adorn the facade. It was designed by Hans Kramer for Dirk Lillie in 1570. The outline of the roof of Chlebnicka Gate (Brama Clebnicka) is in the background.

The huge defensive gate closes Wide Street (ul. Szeroka), and the crane (Żuraw) was the largest port crane in all of medieval Europe (built in 1442-1444). It is equipped with two pairs of wooden drums, 6 and 6.5 meters in diameter, which are put into motion by four workers treading on a staircase which allowed the crane, through a complicated system, to lift a four-ton load to a height of 11 m and two-ton load to 27 m. It was reconstructed after WWII, and currently houses part of the Central Maritime Museum (Centralne Muzeum Morskie).

Ołowianka Island (Wyspa Ołowianka - the name originated from the storage here of non-ferrous metals) is surrounded by the waters of the Old Motława (Stara Motława) and the Stępce Canal (Kanał na Stępce - formerly Ciesielski). In the foreground are the three granaries that were reconstructed for the Central Maritime Museum (Centralne Muzeum Morskie) the **Olive (Oliwski** - fifteenth century), **Copper (Miedź** - nineteenth century) and **Maiden (Panna** - seventeenth century). The old ore and coal carrier **s/s Sołdek**, the first ship built after WWII in the Gdańsk Shipyard in 1948, is moored here. Beyond this stands the Renaissance **Royal Granary (Spichrz Królewski**) built by Jan Strakowski in 1621, and in the background the outline of the former Ołowianka heating factory from 1898 are visible. It was closed in 1997 and has been adapted into a modern concert hall for the Baltic Philharmonic.

The famed ore and coal carrier **s/s Sołdek** is moored at Ołowianka Island. It was launched in the Gdańsk Shipyard on 6 November 1948 and, as the first entirely Polish-built ship to be produced in the post-war period, it became the symbol of the Polish maritime industry. Today, it is a part of the Central Maritime Museum (Centralne Muzeum Morskie) in Gdańsk. The ship was named for a shipyard foreman and tracer from the 1940s and his wife, Helena, was the vessel's godmother.

Just next to this is a piece of Gdańsk's most recent history. A **modern marina** was built in the New Motława (Nowa Motława) basin along the old wharf as part of the Gdańsk Millenium celebrations. It is the first such development within the city limits, and was designed to promote sailing and improve the city's image in the eyes of sailors from western Europe. The area will be further developed to include hotels and other necessary facilities, such as baths, workshops, etc.

The Renaissance **Association of Naturalists House (Dom Towarzystwa Przyrodniczego** - built in 1597) at Długie Pobrzeże, designed by Antoni van Obberghen for the merchant H. Koepe, was one of the tallest patrician houses of its time. It has been owned by the DTP since 1845, and has served as the headquarters of the Museum of Archeology (Muzeum Archeologii) since it was rebuilt after WWII. Primitive figures of early medieval pagan Prussian gods (baby) stand in front of the building. The chief architectural element of the building is the five story alcove and the slim tower with a lamp and a dome is open to the public to see the view from the top. On the right of this building is the St. Mary Gate (Brama Mariacka), a defensive Gothic construction from ca. 1485, which closes ul. Mariacka.

Charming ul. **Mariacka** (whose proper name is **Panieńska** after the Virgin Mary) is closed from the west by the presbytery wall of the monumental St. Mary's Church (Kościół Mariacki) and from the east by the St. Mary Gate (Brama Mariacka). It was almost entirely destroyed at the end of WWII. The original plan of fifteenth century Gothic to nineteenth century Neo-Classicist houses was faithfully reconstructed with porches, cobbles and sewage canals running along the sides of the street. It is often visited by the people of Gdańsk and their guests. Many cafes and souvenir shops line the street to create the unique atmosphere of this intriguing corner of the city.

The fifteenth to nineteenth century **porches (przedproża)** that lined ul. Mariacka were reconstructed from scratch with much of the original stonework, as were the water outlets, named in Polish *rzygacze*, *plwacze* or *gargulce*, all of which carry the connotation of spewing forth water. For centuries, they were part of the specific and unique architecture of Gdańsk and an element of the patrician lifestyle.

The **Gothic Church of the Most Holy Virgin Mary (Kościół Najświętszej Marii Panny** - commonly called **St. Mary's Church (Kościół Mariacki)**, was built in several stages between 1343 and 1502. The nave and the two aisles, the transept and the presbytery have three types of magnificent vaulting. It is the largest brick church in the world with a length of 105.5 m, a width of 48 and 66 m, 28-30 m columns, and an area of ca. 4,900 m^2. The fifteenth to nineteenth century interior, although incomplete, is priceless. The building was rebuilt in 1948-1952, in 1965 it was elevated to the status of Lesser Basilica, and since 1987 it has been the seat of the Gdańsk Diocese. From the top of the tower (76.6 m) there is a fantastic view of the city and its surrounding area. The church's silhouette has become a symbol of the city.

The **main altar** in the presbytery of St. Mary's Church is a late-Gothic polyptych by Master Michał of Augsburg in 1511-1517. The altarpiece (4.89 × 3.90 m) is adorned with monumental figures of God the Father, Mary and Christ seated on a tripartite throne under a canopy. The gold-plated and polychromed group majestically depicts the Coronation of the Virgin. The altarpiece is currently mounted on a rectangular nineteenth century predella decorated with scenes of the Entombment. The moveable wings, filled with either sculpted or painted scenes from the life of Christ, have been largely reconstructed.

The famous **astronomical clock** located on the northern wall of the northern transept sacristy in St. Mary's Church was made by Hans Düringer in 1464-1470, and it is the tallest of its kind in the world (14 m). This clock was in operation until 1553. In 1983-1993 it was reconstructed (70% of elements are original), and now it shows not only the time but the day, month and year, the lunar phase, the positions of the sun and moon in relation to the Zodiac, and others. At noon, scenes of the Annunciation and the Adoration of the Magi appear, the twelve apostles and four evangelists with music playing can be seen in the upper gallery, and Adam and Eve ring bells above them.

The partially preserved 46 chord **organ** in the organ-loft at the western end of St. Mary's Church was made by the master organ builder Marcin Friese in 1625-1629. It is from St. John's Church (Kościół św. Jana) in Gdańsk. Reconstruction of the instrument from 1980-1985 was inspired by Otton Kulcke, a German Gdańsk citizen, and realized by the Harry and Guntram Hillebrandt company from Iserhagen near Hanover. The original Baroque-Mannerist prospect was carved in wood by Peter Brinckmann and Andreas Fischer and polychromed by David van den Block.

The **Royal Chapel** (**Kaplica Królewska**) is the only Baroque sacral building in the historical heart of Gdańsk. Its patrons were King Jan III Sobieski and Primate Andrzej Olszowski, and it was built in 1678-1681 by Bartłomiej Ranisch in cooperation with the sculptor Andrzej Schlüter the Younger (Młodszy) based on a design by Tylman of Gameren. The chapel is the only example of Counter Reformation architecture in Gdańsk.

The early Baroque **Turtle House (Dom Pod Żółwiem** - ul. Św. Ducha 111, formerly 81) dates from 1650. Joanna Schopenhauer lived here. She was the author of a moving diary and the mother of Artur Schopenhauer, the famous philosopher, who was born in 1788 in a nearby house at no. 47, formerly 114).

Salmon House (Dom Pod Łososiem - ul. Szeroka 52), is a Rococo structure from the mid-eighteenth century. From 1704 it was home to the vodka factory and tasting room which had been established by Ambroży Vermoellen w 1598. In was here that the renowned Gdańsk vodka Goldwasser was made. The partially reconstructed interior is today home to an exclusive restaurant.

The damage of 1945 inflicted upon the Gothic hall **church of St. John (Kościół św. Jana)**, dating from the fourteenth and fifteenth centuries, is still being repaired today. A late-Renaissance stone altar from 1599-1612 by Abraham van den Block stands in the church, and the presbytery wall is strongly inclined vertically. The church is currently a concert hall. A charming little lane, one of the characteristic elements of sacral architecture in Gdańsk, encircles the church. This example is the only such fragment that was reconstructed after the destruction of WWII.

The **southern facade** of the Gothic hall **church of St. Nicholas (Kościół św. Mikołaja** – a Lesser Basilica since 1928). It was built in 1348-1390, and expanded in the fifteenth century (tower, sacristy, gables, vaulting). Remnants of the church from 1227-1235, which was most probably built in the place of an even earlier temple from the late twelfth century which had been given to the Dominicans by Prince Świętopełek, can be seen in the sacristy basement. On 11 October 1587 King Zygmunt III Waza received the election act. The rich, Gothic (fifteenth century), Renaissance (sixteenth century), and primarily Baroque and Rococo (seventeenth – eighteenth centuries) interior is original as this church was the only one to have survived WWII untouched.

The fan vaulting system in the nave of the **St. Nichols Basilica (Bazylika św. Mikołaja)** was executed in the early fifteenth century, the chandelier was made in 1617 by Gerd Benningk, the Rococo pews date to ca. 1780, the late-Baroque pulpit dates from 1715 and the seventeenth and eighteenth century altars near the columns are Baroque and Rococo. In the rear of the presbytery there is a colorful arcade with a Gothic crucifix (1520) by Master Paweł situated on the beam. Other elements here include the monumental late-Renaissance main altar from the 1740's with is richly carved and gold-plated with the painting of the Apotheosis of St. Nicholas (Apoteoza św. Mikołaja) by August Ranisch (1643) and the late-Gothic choir stalls from the second half of the fifteenth century with their fabulous backs on which scenes from the life of Christ are depicted.

The octagonal **St. Jacek Bastion** (**Baszta św. Jacka** – named for Jacek Odrowąż, the founder of the Dominican monastery) was built in the late fourteenth century and expanded in the next century. Standing at 36 m, it is the tallest fortification in Gdańsk. The machicolations and brick arcades in the upper part under the roof are original and are supported by stone brackets. The **defensive walls** that extend southerly from the building and run along nearby ul. Podwale Staromiejskie used to be the border between the Main (Główne) and Old (Stare) towns. The neo-Gothic market hall from the late nineteenth century that was built on part of the ruins of a Dominican monastery destroyed by fire in 1813 is visible behind the bastion.

The Jan III Sobieski Monument, dating from 1897 and designed by Tadeusz Barącz, stands at the Wood Market (Targ Drzewny). It had originally stood at Wały Hetmańskie in Lvov, it was moved after 1945 to Wilanów Park, and finally to Gdańsk in 1966. To the east a commemorative plaque on a large granite stone tells us that the square is named after Dariusz Kobzdej, the co-founder in 1979 of the opposition movement known as *Ruch Młodej Polski*.

The Renaissance **Old Town Hall** (**Ratusz Starego Miasta**) was built by Antoni van Obberghen in 1587-1595 and is regarded as one of the most fabulous examples of Gdańsk architecture. The brewer Jan Heweliusz (1611-1687), who later became a famous astronomer and was visited by the Polish kings Jan Kazimierz and Jan III Sobieski and other important people, was also a city councilor and had his office in this building not far from his home on ul. Korzenna. The beautiful interior is original and it houses works of art from other parts of Gdańsk (nineteenth and twentieth centuries).

The fully reconstructed seventeenth century **Miller's Guild (Dom Cechu Młynarzy)** is located on the so-called Tarcza, or island, in the Radunia Canal (Kanał Raduni). Today it is a cafe. The upper part of the western peak of the Great Mill (Wielki Młyn) and the domed tower of St. Catherine's Church (Kościół św. Katarzyny) can both be seen directly behind it.

Almost entirely rebuilt by 1962, the **Great Mill (Wielki Młyn)**, a Gothic construction from ca. 1350, was once one of the largest flour mills in Europe that run on water flowing from the specially built Radunia Canal (ca. 1310) through a system of 18 wheels. It also boasted its own bakery. Today, it is a shopping center, but there is an exhibition in the center which explains how the mill used to work, and a documentary film about the Gdańsk mills can also be viewed.

St. Catherine's Church (Kościół św. Katarzyny), with its three aisles and its separated three-aisled presbytery, is probably the oldest sacred building in Gdańsk. Old-Slavic graves from the tenth to twelfth centuries are in a special crypt in the presbytery. The church was built in stages in the fourteenth and fifteenth centuries. The massive tower is topped with a reconstructed Renaissance dome, known as the Polish type, by Jakub van den Block from 1634. To the east the partially reconstructed presbytery rooftops from the sixteenth century are visible. Inside, 10 types of vaulting combined to create the fabulous ceilings (partly reconstructed). There are also fourteenth and fifteenth century frescoes, a painting from 1510 depicting the *Crucifixion* (*Krzyżowanie*), the late-Gothic altar by St. ??? (św. Erazm) (1515), the Renaissance baptismal font from 1585, the great altar by Szymon Herle (1609-1619) with paintings by Antoni Möller and Izaak van den Block, the Henning epitaph (after 1626), the painting of *Christ Entering Jerusalem* (*Wjazd Chrystusa do Jerozolimy*) by Bartłomiej Milwitz (1654), and others.

The tradition of the **carillon** (**karylon**), the set of 49 bells that hang in the tower of **St. Catherine's Church** (**Kościół św. Katarzyny**), dates to the sixteenth century. Until 1999, it was under renovation as part of the unity and friendship program between the Polish and German nations. The tower also houses the Museum of Tower Clocks (Muzeum Zegarów Wieżowych).

The epitaph of Jan Heweliusz (**Epitafium Jana Heweliusza**) in the presbytery of St. Catherine's Church (Kościół św. Katarzyny) was made by the Berlin sculptor Meyer in 1779. Its patron was Daniel G. Dawidson, whose maternal great-grandfather had been the famous Gdańsk astronomer. The tombstone that Heweliusz paid for himself (which used to be in the same location beneath the floor) is next to the pillar with the epitaph. A special case holds a small plaque which was removed from atop the astronomer's coffin.

St. Bridget's Church (Kościół św. Brygidy) was built in the fourteenth and fifteenth centuries on the site of a former convent, and it was expanded at the beginning of the sixteenth century. It is a hall church with three aisles and a separated presbytery. The tower was built by Bartel Ranisch in 1604 and the dome by Piotr Willer is from 1673. Almost entirely rebuilt in 1971-1975, it has been the shrine of shipyard Solidarność since 1980, and the crosses that have been associated with strikes are displayed here. It has been a Lesser Basilica since 1993. The mostly modern interior was designed by Elżbieta Szczodrowska, Robert Pepliński and Bohdan Pietruszka. Interesting old works of art include the paintings *Allegory of the Triumphant Church* (*Alegoria Triumfującego Kościoła*) by Herman Han (second half of the sixteenth century) and the colorful *Crucifixion* (*Ukrzyżowanie*) from the seventeenth century.

The **monstrance** in St. Bridget's Church (Kościół św. Brygidy), impressive in size at a height of 174 cm and a weight of about 30 kg, was made of gold, silver and amber by Mariusz Drapikowski in 2000.

The metal sculpture of the **Monument to the Defenders of the Polish Post Office (Pomnik Obrońców Poczty Polskiej)** was designed by Wacław Kućma and Krystyna Heyde-Kućma in 1979 and stands on the square in front of the post office to commemorate the 14-hour heroic defense of the Polish post office on 1 September 1939. The building still houses the post office, and also the Museum of Post and Telecommunications (Muzeum Poczty i Telekomunikacji). In the courtyard, there is an interesting bronze bas-relief designed by Zygfryd Korpalski depicting the tragedy of the heroic postal clerks.

The **Gothic St. James's Church** (**Kościół św. Jakuba** – ul. Łagiewniki) has a single aisle and was built in 1432-1437 on the site of a sailors' chapel. The upper part of the tower dates from 1639. In the nineteenth century, an ave-bell from the seventeenth century St. James Gate (Brama św. Jakuba) was hung in the church tower. Destroyed in 1945, it was rebuilt by the Capuchin order and it obtained a modern interior.

The **Monument to the Fallen Shipyard Workers** (**Pomnik Poległych Stoczniowców**) was built in 1981 on Solidarność Square in front of Gate no. 2 of the Gdańsk Shipyard to commemorate the heroic shipyard workers and the tragedies they suffered in 1970 and 1980. It is composed of three 48 m tall crosses made of ship steel with three anchors hung from the crosses transverses (designed B. Pietruszka). The lower parts of the crosses are decorated with scenes from the lives of the shipyard workers by E. Szczodrowska and R. Pepliński.

The neo-Renaissance **PKP Main Railway Station (Dworzec Główny PKP)** was built after the defensive walls were razed 1895-1900. The building is dominated by the 48 m water tower with a dome based on the design of the one at the Main Town Hall (Ratusz Głównego Miasta). The renovation of the interior (1995-1997) aroused much controversy, and has become an example of the contempt of the user towards artistically valuable open spaces.

Corpus Christi Church (**Kościół Bożego Ciała**), built on the site of a hospital outside the old city walls, combines the modesty of the Gothic (main hall 1395-1465) and the Baroque (side aisles 1687-1688, tower 1750-1765). The interior includes a late-Baroque main altar (1768), an organ (1766-1768) made by Friedrich R. Dalitz, a painted ceiling (currently in very poor condition) from 1709 by Carl F. Falckenberg and other elements. A place to commemorate the Gdańsk cemeteries that were liquidated after WWII is planned next to the church.

The middle caponier, blockhouse and the counterscarp gallery that form part of the ***Grodzisko* Fort** (located behind the PKS bus station) date from 1807-1814 and 1867-1874. This is a good place to contemplate and admire the nineteenth century art of fortification building. Vicious battles for Gdansk fought by the Russian, Saxon and Napoleon armies took place here in 1734 and 1807. The site was expanded in the seventeenth century, although it had been used as a defensive position as early as the middle ages. A 20 m tall metal cross was placed on the Grodzisko in 2000. There is a great view of Gdańsk from this vantage point.

St. Elizabeth's Church (**Kościół św. Elżbiety** – late fourteenth century) is a single aisle Gothic church built on the site of a former hospital. It has an interesting suspended tower above the entrance, and its presbytery was added by August Stüler in 1846. From the second half of the sixteenth century it was Calvinistic, and later (1846) it became a garrison church. Its modest interior includes a stained-glass window made by Zofia Baudouin de Courtenay in 1952.

The Franciscan **Church of the Holy Trinity (Kościół św. Trójcy** – 1481-1514) is a Gothic three-aisled hall church with beautiful gables, that separate the eastern side the reading room, a rarity in Poland, from the earlier presbytery (formerly the Church of the Lord's Supper (Kościół Wieczerzy Pańskiej) from 1422-1431). The Chapel of St. Ann (kaplica św. Anny – 1480-1484), designated for Poles, is located on the southern side of the church. To the church's north is the residential Pulpit House (Dom Kazalnicowy) that was built based on skeleton construction. The main church interior includes nine Gothic stalls (1510-1511), a Renaissance pulpit (1541), the epitaph of the Marquis Giovanne B. B. d' Oria (1597), the wonderful spider (1653) and other works. The chapel interior has an altar, an loft with an organ (1710), a pulpit (1721) and an altar painting of the *Return of the Prodigal Son* (*Powrót syna marnotrawnego* – seventeenth century). To the south is the former monastery building (1481-1514), once a part of this large monastic complex, which functioned as a school (1558), was home to the famous Academic Gymnasium (Gimnazjum Akademickie – 1580), and later became a museum (1872). Today, it houses the Gdańsk Branch of the National Museum (Muzeum Narodowe). The ground floor houses permanent exhibits of Gdańsk furniture, altars, sculpture, wood carvers grates, china, garments, liturgical ornaments, etc., an extensive collection of paintings from fifteenth to twentieth centuries is located on the first floor, and the second floor is used for temporary exhibitions.

The famous Gothic **triptych of the _Last Judgement_** (**Sąd Ostateczny**) by the renowned Flemish painter Hans Memling (1472 - 1473) is the most valuable work in the collections of the Gdańsk Branch of the National Museum (on loan from St. Mary's Church). The paintings patrons, the Italian Angelo Tani and his wife Catherine - with ties to the Medici family, are depicted on the exterior of the side wings that are visible when the triptych is closed (photograph to follow).

The **Bastion of St. Gertrude (Bastion św. Gertrudy)** closes the western end of the defensive fortifications of old Gdańsk (designed by Antoni van Obberghen and built at the end of the sixteenth century) are patterned after neo-Italianate fortifications. Next to this is the **Bison Bastion (Bastion Żubr** - correctly Aurochs (Tur) that was built in the Dutch manner by Corneliusz van der Bosch in 1621-1629. These two structures are surrounded by a wonderful view of the city, the edge of the Gdańsk Heights (Wysoczyzna Gdańska), the residential quarters of Zaroślak, Nowe Szkoty and Orunia, and bastions, moats and the Żuławy Gdańskie area.

The **stone sluice** is an singularly outstanding hydrotechnical project in European terms. It was designed and built by Willem J. Benning and Adrian Olbrants in 1619-1624. The lock regulates the water level in the Motława River and in the moats. The ruins of a grain water mill stand next to it.

The **Church of SS. Peter and Paul** (**Kościół św. Piotra i Pawła**) at ul. Żabi Kruk is the former parish church of the Old Suburb (Stary Przedmieścia) that was built in 1397 and expanded in 1456. From 1486 to 1514, its walls were heightened and a tower with a large roof and finished with stepped gables was built to the west. Its interior houses tombstones and the Uphagen Chapel. One of the side chapels holds the painting of The Gracious Virgin (Matka Boska Łaskawa) from Stanisławów that was once the object of cult adoration by Armenians (eighteenth century).

The **Wisłoujście Fortress**, unique on a European scale, once protected the Vistula River mouth through which ships sailed into the Gdańsk port on the Motława River. The lighthouse tower from 1482 was later surrounded by walls, towers and moats reminds visitors of the great maritime city Gdańsk once was.

Westerplatte, where WWII began, is the site of the 25 meter high **Monument to the Defenders of the Coast (Pomnik Obrońców Wybrzeża)** built of 224 granite blocks weighing a total weight of 1,150 tons. It can be seen from afar, and serves as a good orientation point in the city landscape. It commemorates the Polish sailors and soldiers who fought on all the WWII fronts.

The **barracks** in Westerplatte, built in 1935-38, was designed to be a defensive construction and, at the time, it was a real achievement of Polish military architecture with flexible floors, a self-supporting construction, masking, etc. It was destroyed by the communist authorities in 1947.

Jaśkowa Dolina is a charming part of the Gdańsk district of Wrzeszcz. It was once a favorite place for walks, relaxation and outdoor games for the rich of Gdansk, who began building summer residences (palaces) here in the seventeenth century.

The **Gutenberg Grove (Gaj Gutenberga)** with a gazebo and statue (reconstructed) is located near Jaśkowa Dolina on a moraine hill. It was built in the late-nineteenth century by the Gdańsk Printers' Guild (Gdański Cech Drukarzy) to commemorate Johannes Gutenberg, the inventor of the press. A copy of his original work, the famous Gutenberg Bible from ca. 1455, is kept in the Diocese Museum (Muzeum Diecezjalne) in Pelplin, a small town near Gdańsk.

A detail of the Gdańsk Przymorze housing estate, erected in the early 1970s. The ten-story **wave-shaped (falowiec) apartment blocks** are characteristic to this development. The block on ul. Obrońców Wybrzeża is approximately 850 m long and the other on ul. Jagiellońska is about 800 m long.

The pier in Brzeźno that opened in 1997, along with bike-paths and promenades, has long been a favorite recreational area for the residents of the nearby Gdańsk quarters of Zaspa, Nowy Port and Przymorze.

***Pachołek* hill** (100.8 m above sea level), close to the Oliwa Cathedral, was most likely once a cult site for Pomeranian pagans, has been known as a vantage point since the late eighteenth century. From atop the 20 m platform, erected in 1975, a beautiful view spreads from Sopot, the Gulf of Gdańsk, Oliwa and other Gdańsk quarters, the Gdańsk Heights (Wysoczyzna Gdańska) and the Valley of Joy (Dolina Radości). The layout of the Cistercian abbey in Oliwa, including the church and monastery to the south, the two abbey palaces, the park and grange, and the parish church of St. James (św Jakuba), is especially clear.

The famous post-Cistercian **Church of the Holy Trinity, St. Mary and St. Bernard (Kościół św. Trójcy, NMP and św. Bernarda)** has been commonly referred to as Oliwa Cathedral since the inception of the Diocese of Gdańsk here in 1926. It has been a Lesser Basilica since 1971. The 107 m long building is three-aisled with a transverse nave, a presbytery and an ambulatory. Traces of different architectural styles, from the Romanesque oratory (ca. 1200) to twentieth century elements, can be seen throughout the church. Its rich decoration also originates from various periods from the fifteenth to the twentieth centuries.

The Rococo **main organ** in the Oliwa Cathedral (Katedra Oliwska) with its 110 chords, and 7,876 organ-pipes, is the outstanding work of the Cistercian monk Michał (Jan W. Wulf of Orneta) dating from 1763-1788. It was completed by the master organist Friedrich R. Dalitz in 1791-1793. Its fantastic semi-elliptical prospect, a rarity in Europe, with statues of angles, movable trumpets and trombones, suns and stars was made in a local workshop under the supervision of the brothers Alanus and Józef Gross.

The late-Renaissance **altar of the Holy Trinity (ołtarz św. Trójcy)** on the eastern wall of the northern wing of the transverse nave in the Oliwa Cathedral is a marvelous example of the local Cistercian workshop which was well-known in Poland for many years. Its patron was Rafał Kos, a Cistercian monk from Oliwa. The altar from 1606 has three levels and is richly decorated with sculptures, paintings and especially polychromes made by Wolfgang Sporer (Spor).

The patron of the **tomb of the Pomeranian Princes tomb** (**grobowiec książąt pomorskich**) of 1615 was Abbot Dawid Konarski. Made of black marble and featuring an image of a griffin, it stands in the northern transept of the Oliwa Cathedral and once covered the entrance to the crypt in the presbytery where the ashes of east-Pomeranian Princes and their family members still rest.

A late-Baroque **pulpit** in Oliwa Cathedral, from the second half of the eighteenth century, is located to the left of the presbytery. It was made in a local workshop, its walls are decorated with panels featuring scenes from the life and works of St. Bernard, and the acoustic canopy is decorated with figures.

The Baroque **main altar** in the presbytery of Oliwa Cathedral is from 1688 and its patron was Abbot Michał A. Hacki. The 7 m tall colonnade is its main feature, in the middle of which is an Andreas Stech painting *The Adoration of Mary with Admirers* (*Adoracja Marii z adorantami*). Above the colonnade's entablature is a concave space made of stucco and decorated with a starry sky, approximately 150 heads of angels, and characters from both the Old and New Testaments.

The new **Abbots' Palace** (**Pałac Opatów**), behind the lawns and flower-beds in the French part of Oliwa Park is surrounded by four trimmed yews from the second half of the eighteenth century. The palace was built in the seventeenth century, later to be expanded by Abbot Józef J. Rybiński in 1754-1756. It was rebuilt after being destroyed by fire in 1945, and it has been home to a museum since 1926.

The alley formed by specially shaped trees whose branches and leaves create a roof, is in the northern part of Oliwa Park (Park Oliwski), is adjacent to the eastern pond which is an extension of the famous Linden-tree Lane (Aleja Lipowa). The park's origins date to the sixteenth or seventeenth centuries. The Cistercian Abbot Rybiński ordered the park to be redesigned in 1760, and the new park was built in the French style by Kazimierz Dębiński from Kock, who had designed the Wilanów Park. By 1792, the park had been expanded on its northern side, and the new area was laid out in the English style by Johannes G. Salzmann.

118

The **pier** in the town of Sopot, once a fishing village and since the nineteenth century also a spa, obtained its current shape and length (516 m) in 1927. It consists of three main parts: the platform at the base of the pier, which is used for sunbathing, the main pedestrian promenade and a side wing (ca. 130 m), perfect for sunbathing and inhaling the iodine-filled air. The pier is a place every tourist must visit.

The **fountain** located opposite the base of the pier is an important historic monument. Built before the First World War, it impressed the public with its colorful illumination and its great height of over 20 m. The area surrounding it, including the Spa-house, medicinal baths, concert shell and promenade were modernized in the 1930s, only to be significantly changed after WWII.

Currently **The Heroes of the Monte Cassino Street (ulica im. Bohaterów Monte Cassino)** "Monciak", as it is called, is not just a fashionable promenade. Until the nineteenth century, it was one of the main streets of the fishing village of Sopot that led from the sea to a grange located near aleja Niepodległości. It also provided coastal access for the summer houses of rich Gdańsk families who were as eager to take advantage of the bathing the sea offered, something which is still popular today. The commander-in-chief Jan Sobieski and his wife Marysieńka were among those who took bathing cures at the beach in nearby Kolibki.

The **Forest Opera (Opera Leśna)** is today the unquestionable symbol of Sopot, and a monument to Polish song, although the current theater is nothing like the original. The small forest valley with great natural acoustics was discovered in the late nineteenth century. During the summer season spa visitors eagerly walked up here to listen to special solo concerts. The first professional concert theater was built in 1909and renowned Wagner festivals took place here. The theater has been modernized many times since WWII, especially to facilitate TV transmissions. The light-weight canopy which stretches over the audience of five thousand was added in 1961. Today, the theater is fully modernized, and the primary advantages of the site, its natural acoustics, are neither known nor even important.

Sopot's **Grand Hotel** (formerly the **Casino Hotel**) was built in 1924-1927. This distinctive hotel is located almost directly on the beach, and has hosted many important people, politicians, artists and businessmen, and its most famous room is the General's Apartment (Apartament Generalski) in which General Charles de Gaulle stayed. As in every respected hotel, there is no room 13.

Gdynia port construction, 1923. The s/s Kentucky, which sailed from here in 1923 carrying immigrants to the USA, was the first ship to ever sail into the port of Gdynia and moor at the wooden pier. Gdynia, just like Sopot, had been just a fishing village for centuries. It was owned by the Cistercians from Oliwa until the nineteenth century. The unexpected development of the village into a city was forced by the geographical situation of the newly created Second Commonwealth (Druga Rzeczypospolita). Access to the Baltic Sea and the need for a modern port were the subject of much debate, and Minister Eugeniusz Kwiatkowski chose Gdynia and was successful in defending his choice. The Polish Parliament decree of 23 September 1922 signaled the beginning of the great construction project, which has continued practically to the present day. Gdynia often serves as an example of modern Poland during the interwar period.

The **Church of the Blessed Virgin Mary** (**Kościół Najświętszej Marii Panny** - ca. 1932) in Gdynia. The buildings along ul. Świętojańska, the busy center, modern office buildings and port traffic are all inherent to the ever growing city.

From the vantage point at **Stone Hill (Kamienna Góra)** (52.4 m above sea level) one can see the General M. Zaruski yacht harbor, the outer part of the port and the South Pier, the breakwater, the roadstead in the Gulf of Gdańsk, the Hel Peninsula in good weather, and the housing estates of Gdynia. The once small Kashubian village has been a dynamically developing city since 1920.

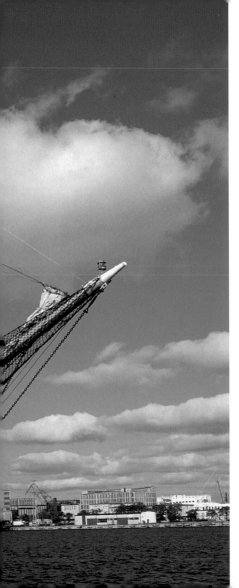

The **tall-ship *Dar Pomorza*** is moored at the Pomeranian Quay of the South Pier (Nabrzeże Pomorskie Mola Południowego) and is today a museum. Previously, it was a training ship for the Maritime Academy, and it sailed around the world many times carrying students and future officers of the merchant fleet. The ship played an important educational role for the crew of the Polish fleet, and when it was retired, due to age and technical state, it was replaced with the very similar modern sailing ship. ***Dar Młodzieży***. As a matter of fact, youths from all over Poland contributed financially to the building of the ship which the Gdynia Maritime Academy owns.

Kościuszko Square (Skwer Kościuszki) and the South Pier (Molo Południowe) form a beautiful open area, and it is not a coincidence that several important Gdynia monuments are located here. The fountain, built in the 1970s, is special with its sea-green water and its original illumination.

Ulica Świętojańska is the most important street in Gdynia and nearly a promenade. To the left is the Church of the Blessed Virgin Mary (Kościół Najświętszej Marii Panny) (not pictured). During the years of communist stagnation, the small shops that were located here, supplied with western goods by returning sailors, was a window on the world for the entire Tri-Cities.

The first **pier** (175 m - partially reconstructed) **in Orłowo**, currently a district of Gdynia, was built in 1934 as a landing for the Vistula Ship Company that sailed between Tczew and Gdynia. The tall cliff that rises above the shore is a part of the Redłowo Hillock (Kępa Redłowska - 90.8 m above sea level), a protected nature preserve which includes the shoreline.

Orłowo is a slightly sleepy residential area of Gdynia which was enlivened by the building of *Klif*, **a modern shopping mall**, where many people from Gdynia and Sopot meet.